Famous
Illustrated Tales of
RAMAYANA

MAPLE KIDS

Famous Illustrated Tales of
RAMAYANA

Published by

MAPLE PRESS PRIVATE LIMITED

Corporate & Editorial Office
A 63, Sector 58, Noida 201 301, U.P., India

phone: +91 120 455 3581, 455 3583
email: info@maplepress.co.in
website: www.maplepress.co.in

Reprint 2020

ISBN: 978-93-88304-37-5

Illustration by Artyfino
Printed at HT Media Limited, Gr. Noida, India

10 9 8 7 6 5 4 3

Contents

The Birth of Rama

King Dasaratha of Suryavansh ruled over the beautiful kingdom of Kosala. Ayodhya, a city along the river Sarayu, was the capital of Kosala. It was a land of peace and prosperity. The city was beautiful with magnificent buildings, neat rows of houses, broad, clean roads and splendid gardens. The people of Ayodhya were happy and contented. King Dasaratha was gifted with valour, glory and fame.

He had three wives: Kausalya, Kaikeyi and Sumitra. Though they had everything they wanted, they did not have any children. This was the biggest sorrow of the King and his queens.

As the years rolled by, King Dasaratha's sorrow became a cause of worry for there was no one to succeed his throne. He sought his Guru Vasishtha's advice who after deep thought, advised him to conduct a 'Puthrakameshti Yagna'. It was a sacrifice performed to please the Gods to have children to which Dasaratha agreed.

During the same time, the Gods went to Lord Vishnu, the sustainer of the world, to save them from Ravana who had caused destruction on Earth. Ravana, the demon king had been blessed by Lord Shiva. Lord Vishnu promised them that he himself would go down to Earth and kill Ravana,

taking the human form of Prince Rama. At the Yagna, Dasaratha made offerings to the Fire God and pleased him. Finally, 'Agnideva' or the 'God of Fire' appeared in front of Dasaratha and handed over a bowl of sweet, saying, "Dasaratha! I am pleased with your prayers. Here's a bowl of *kheer*. Distribute this among your wives and they will be blessed with sons!" Agnideva then vanished.

King Dasaratha handed over the kheer to his wives, Kausalya and Kaikeyi. They both had half of the *kheer* and shared half of their remaining share each with Sumitra. Thus, all the queens had their share of the kheer.

In the course of time, the three queens gave birth to boys. Kausalya and Kaikeyi gave birth to Rama and Bharatha respectively whereas Sumitra gave birth to the twins – Lakshmana and Shatrugna. King Dasaratha and the entire Ayodhya rejoiced at the birth of the four Princes and wore a festive look.

As time passed, the four princes grew up together with love and affection. They were excellent in their academics, wisdom and wit. They were also trained in the humanities, science, arts, scriptures and also the art of warfare. They were very well guided by their Guru and therefore, became brave, noble and virtuous.

Soon, the news about the noble qualities of the boys began to reach far and wide. Sage Vishwamitra, who himself was a powerful king once, was impressed with the princes. He had given up his worldly pleasures and had gone to the forest to do penance where he acquired the blessings of Lord Shiva and was granted all the divine weapons. Vishwamitra felt that those weapons should reach the right person. As he knew that Rama was a divine incarnation of Vishnu, who had come to the world to destroy evil, he went to meet Dasaratha and his princes.

Vishwamitra's Advent

When Vishwamitra arrived at the court of Dasaratha, he felt honoured to receive the sage but at the same time, Dasaratha became anxious for he knew that Sage Vishwamitra was short-tempered. To make him angry would mean a curse. After paying his due respects to the sage, Dasaratha called his sons to take the blessings of the sage.

Vishwamitra said, "King Dasaratha! I am pleased by your hospitality but you did not ask me why I have come to you! I have come to seek your help."

Dasaratha told the sage with humble respect, "Respectable Guru! I am honoured by your visit. And, to give you my services is my duty. Please let me know the purpose of your visit."

Vishwamitra replied, "O King! I am happy to hear this and to see your boys. I have heard about their great skills so I have come here to ask you to send your elder son, Rama with me!"

Surprised by Vishwamitra's words, King Dasaratha bowed to the sage and requested, "O great Sage! I promise to do whatever you wish me to do. I will be happy to send my son with you. But first tell me about your mission please."

Vishwamitra said calmly, "Dasaratha!

I want to perform a yagna but the demons in the forest - Tadaka, Subahu and Maricha are creating terror. They control the Dandaka Forest, which was once beautiful, but now is a frightening place because of them. After a long thought, I came to the conclusion that only Rama can fight with them and kill them."

Hearing this, King Dasaratha was devastated. He could not think of Rama going to the forest with Vishwamitra. He fell down on the ground. When he regained consciousness after some time, he prayed to Vishwamitra with folded hands and said, "O Great Sage! Rama is too young for your mission. If you want, I am ready to come to help you. I can handle any powerful demon and defeat him."

Hearing these words, Sage Vishwamitra became angry. He thundered, "Dasaratha! You had promised me that you would do what I ask of you but now you are saying you cannot! Do you know how you would be cursed if you go back on your words?"

At this, Dasaratha became frightened as there was every chance of him being cursed by Vishwamitra if he did not keep his promise. At the same time, Rama was very dear to his heart. He could not think of a day without Rama. Also, the risk of Rama's life in danger put him in a fix.

Sage Vasishtha, who was watching him, calmed him down and said, "Dasaratha! Do not worry about sending Rama. He is very brave and is capable of fighting any powerful force. In fact, he alone can slay the forest demons but you should send Lakshmana along. They both can fight the demons and would bring success and glory to you."

King Dasaratha was relieved at this and agreed to send his sons with Vishwamitra.

When Rama and Lakshmana were told about their mission with Vishwamitra, they became excited. They bowed to their parents and guru and followed Vishwamitra.

It was a long expedition. They had to cross River Ganga before they could reach the Dandaka forest. During their journey, Vishwamitra related the story of Tadaka and her sons.

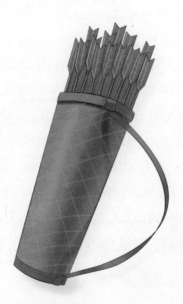

Tadaka and Subahu's Assassination

Both the princes continued walking in the forest with the sage. They stopped at a place where the rivers, Saryu and Ganges met. They crossed the river in a boat. After that they reached another dense forest. They could hear the sounds of animals and birds. The sage said, "The forest is essentially a peaceful area except from the danger of Tadaka and her sons."

Suketu, a powerful Yaksha, performed a penance for a son. Pleased with him, Lord Brahma offered him a boon that he would have a child. Suketu brought up Tadaka like a son as she was blessed with the strength of thousand elephants. Since he wanted a son, Tadaka married Sunda and had two sons, Maricha and Subahu. Once, Sunda irked Sage Agastya, so the sage cursed him to death. Angered with this, Tadaka and Maricha troubled the sage, who cursed them too that she and Maricha would become demons. Since then, Tadaka ,Maricha and Subahu began to destroy the beautiful forest and frightened those who came there.

It was almost evening when the three stepped into Tadakavana. They were stopped by a thundering voice which said, "Who is that coming to my area? How dare you come here?"

Sage Vishwamitra and the boys looked around. In front of them suddenly appeared a huge, ugly creature, who was Tadaka. The boys and their Guru continued to walk towards her. Tadaka threw big boulders towards them while Rama and Lakshmana aimed their arrows at her. Although, Tadaka's hands were cut which made her cry in pain, she got ready for a counter attack when Sage Vishwamitra ordered Rama, "Come on Rama! Don't delay! Aim at her heart."

As Rama aimed at her heart, the arrow pierced her heart, making her fall dead. Magically, the next moment, Tadakavana turned into a colourful and beautiful Dandaka Forest, as it was before. Vishwamitra was pleased and gave Rama, all his divine weapons, including the Brahmastra.

The trio then reached Vishwamitra's hermitage, Siddhashrama. The next day, a sacrifice was planned by Vishwamitra for the next six days. The sage instructed the boys that the yagna would be attended by some more sages, and accordingly, they should keep a watch over the demons who may try to disturb them.

The next day, the princes woke up early and started their watch. However, the yagna went on without any disturbance. To Vishwamitra and the others' surprise, the next and the subsequent four days of the yagna also went on without any disturbance.

When the yagna proceeded to the sixth day, the most important day of the yagna, a terrible sound of roaring laughter was suddenly heard. As Rama and the others looked up, they found Maricha and his brother Subahu, along with many other demons in the sky. They started throwing flesh, blood, meat, bones etc. onto the people around the sacrificial fire. Rama fired his Manavastra which hit Maricha on his chest and hurled him several miles away, into the ocean while the Agniastra hit Subahu and burnt him to death. Seeing their fate, the other demons started running helter-skelter in panic. Rama and Lakshmana chased them with successive arrows, which killed them all. The brothers' victory was hailed by rain of flowers from the Gods. The yagna then proceeded and was successfully completed. Vishwamitra was proud of the princes and celebrated the victory with joy. He and the other sages blessed the brothers.

The Wedding

The next morning, Sage Vishwamitra told the princes that they would proceed to the city of Mithila, the capital of the Kingdom of Janaka. He told them that King Janaka had invited him to perform a yagna and he wanted Rama to marry Sita, King Janaka's beautiful daughter. She was known to be the incarnation of Goddess Lakshmi.

King Janaka had arranged for a 'swayamvara' for Sita to select the strongest and bravest groom. Kings, princes and sages from all over the land had come to attend the 'swayamvara'. He had announced that the one who could string the 'bow' would be eligible to marry Sita. The big, strong and heavy bow was the 'Shiva Dhanush', a divine gift given to him by Lord Shiva.

On their journey towards Mithila, the trio came across the hermitage of Sage Gautama. They saw a big stone outside, which was actually Ahilya, who had been cursed by Gautama for her infidelity. She had become a stone and would only get back to her old self at the touch of Rama's foot. So, Vishwamitra told Rama to touch the stone with his feet. When Rama did so, the stone turned into Ahilya, who offered warm hospitality to them.

At Mithila, the people were thrilled to see the Princes. One of Sita's maids told her about Rama's charm. When Sita had a glimpse of Rama, they both were carried away by each other's charm, and wished to marry each other.

On reaching the palace, Sage Vishwamitra introduced Rama and Lakshmana to King Janaka.

During the 'Swayamwara', the Kings and Princes from several kingdoms tried to string the bow, but failed. No one could even move it! Vishwamitra then gestured Rama to try it. Taking his blessings, Rama lifted the bow with one hand and placed it against his toe. He then pulled the string to the other end. To everyone's surprise, the bow snapped into two with a thunderous sound with the entire court going into applause.

The tremendous noise reached the ears of Lord Parashurama who was meditating on the top of the Mahendra Mountains. Being an ardent devotee of Lord Shiva, he was extremely angry to know that the pious 'Shiv Dhanush' had been broken. He went to the royal court of Janak and rebuked Rama for breaking the bow. But when Rama sincerely apologized to him, his anger subsided and he showered the beautiful couple with his blessings.

Sita, who had been watching everything from the balcony, was relieved. Rama too felt very delighted. King Janaka and Vishwamitra were overjoyed that

Rama and Sita would become a perfect couple. They sent messengers to King Dasaratha to break this joyful news and invite him for the wedding.

Dasaratha's joys knew no bounds when he heard about the progress of his sons, and the union of Rama with Sita. Thus, he started his journey to Mithila with his royal retinue.

Not only did Rama marry Sita, Rama's brothers too were married to Sita's sisters. Thus, Lakshmana married Urmila, Bharatha married Mandavi and Shatrugna married Shrutakirti. The marriage took place with pomp and show. Both the cities of Ayodhya and Mithila wore a festive look to celebrate the grand marriages. After the marriage ceremony, the couples took the blessings of all their elders and returned to Ayodhya.

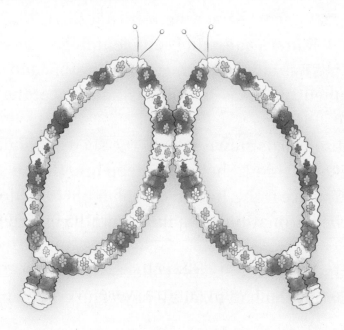

Rama's Coronation

Few months later, King Dasaratha consulted sage Vasishtha, and his minister and decided to make his beloved son, Rama, ascend the throne. Vasishtha fixed the next day for the coronation and King Dasaratha gave orders for the preparations of the ceremony. While, the entire kingdom started the preparations and cheered the decision, Bharatha and Shatrugna were away at their uncle's place and did not know about the happy occasion.

But, Manthara, the hunch-backed maid of queen Kaikeyi was not happy about the news. She rushed to Kaikeyi who too was happy about Rama's coronation, for she loved him more than Bharatha.

Manthara said to her, "Oh Kaikeyi! I pity you! If Rama can become the King, why not Bharatha? He too is of Rama's age, and is efficient in governance. The King has sidelined you and Bharatha, and very conveniently, he has sent Bharatha away at the right time!"

These words slowly sowed the seeds of doubt in Kaikeyi's mind. She took a deep breath and said, "Yes! You are right. It is an evil plan but how do I stop the coronation of Rama? Bharatha is also not here!"

Manthara said, "Just recollect when years ago, Dasaratha had to face a powerful enemy in a

battle. You were there with him and saved the life of the king. He was pleased with you and was ready to give you two boons. You said you would have them when you need it. Kaikeyi, this is the right time. Ask for those two boons: first, Bharatha should be crowned the King, and second, Rama should be sent on an exile to the forest for fourteen years as after fourteen years, he would not claim ownership to the Kingdom!"

Dumbstruck at this perfect idea, Kaikeyi waited for Dasaratha's arrival.

When Dasaratha came, he found Kaikeyi lying down on the floor with her hair dishevelled and her ornaments strewn. Shocked, he asked her, "Kaikeyi! Are you not getting ready for the festivity?"

Kaikeyi said, "Oh! But first tell me, have you forgotten the boons that you promised me?"

Confused about the relevance of such a question, Dasaratha said, "No Kaikeyi! I am ready to fulfil them any time but right now, let us get ready for the coronation."

However, Kaikeyi firmly said, "No! You have to first consider my boons and then the coronation."

Left with no other option, Dasaratha asked what she wanted.

When Kaikeyi told him about his two wishes, Dasaratha's heart sank for a second. He felt the whole world crumbling before him. Then he stuttered, "But... but... why?"

Kaikeyi insisted, "Will you break your promise? Are you not righteous?"

King Dasaratha was in a fix. He held his head and sat down to calm himself. What should he choose: his love for Rama or his sense of justice towards his promise? Finally he declared, "Alright Kaikeyi! I grant you the boons. Send a word for Rama!"

When Rama came to Kaikeyi's chamber, Dasaratha told him about his decision with a heavy heart. However, Rama, having understood his father's feelings, held his hands and said, "Father, bless me. I am ready to go to exile."

Rama's Exile to the Forest

When Lakshmana entered the chamber of the queen, he became furious as he had overheard the conversation but remained quiet as he looked at Rama. When the news spread about Rama's exile, the people of Ayodhya were shocked. Kausalya was inconsolable. However, Rama consoled them all and seeked their blessings.

When he came to Sita, she too was in tears. Rama said, "Sita! Be a good daughter –in- law for my parents. Take care of them till I return." Sita replied, "Do you think I can live without you? Is it not then my duty to follow your footsteps? "

Rama intervened, "But Sita, I would be going to the forest. It would be difficult for you to stay there for fourteen years."

But Sita was unconvinced and said, " When you are around, I can withstand any hardship. Please take me along." Rama had no other option but to agree.

When the news of Sita accompanying Rama reached Lakshmana, he came running to them and said, "You are like my parents. How can a child live without his parents? Please, let me also come with you. Let me be a guard to you both." Rama was moved by Lakshmana's words and immediately agreed. Rama, Lakshmana and Sita, changed their royal outfits to ascetic clothes, and went to Dasaratha to take his blessings.

Dasaratha said to Rama, "Son! Please change your mind. I cannot stay alive if you leave me!" Rama soothed him, "Father! Your promise to mother Kaikeyi should not be broken. I have always abided by my mother's instructions. Please let me do my duty as your son. I would come back to you after fourteen years."

Having realized that Rama was in no way to change his mind, Dasaratha blessed them. He then ordered his ministers to arrange for their departure, accompanied by an army, along with horses, elephants.

The entire Ayodhya gathered to see off their beloved princes. There were tears in their eyes and pain in their hearts. However, Rama was calm and composed, as he took their leave. Driven by Sumantara, the chariot reached the banks of River Tamasa, followed by the people. It was evening by then, so the trio as well as the people stopped to rest. Well before the dawn, Rama told Sumantara to drive the chariot across the border, when the people were still asleep. They reached the banks of River Ganga, where they were welcomed by the tribal chief, Guha. He was too excited and felt honoured to have Rama at his place. Rama asked him to ferry them across the river.

Guha, however said, "Oh noble soul! First let me wash your feet with my hands. That would be the biggest honour to me." That being done, Rama took leave from Sumantara while Guha ferried the trio in his boat.

Bharatha's Homecoming

Meanwhile in Ayodhya, King Dasaratha's condition worsened. He hoped that Sumantara would have persuaded Rama and the others to come back. His eyes eagerly looked everywhere for his beloved children when Sumantara entered his chamber. When Sumantara explained to the king that the trio was left at the riverbanks, Dasaratha's heart became heavy with guilt and he went into a swoon, never to wake up again.

Word was sent to Bharatha and Shatrugna to return to Ayodhya immediately. They were totally puzzled to see the entire kingdom in gloom and by the way they were greeted by the people. They were stunned to find absolute silence everywhere.

When Bharatha entered his mother's chamber, Kaikeyi was overjoyed to see him. She hugged him and asked him, "Oh my dear son! Welcome home! How are uncle and grandfather? I'm so glad to see you!"

But Bharatha became restless and inquired about his brothers and father.

Kaikeyi calmly said, "Keep calm, my son!

Your father is safe in Heaven. He has bestowed you the crown!" In utter shock, Bharatha said, "What? You mean my father is no more? But how? And where are my brothers, Rama and Lakshmana?"

As Bharatha grew impatient, Kaikeyi explained everything to her son, hoping that he would appreciate her act. But Bharatha was very angry and screamed, "You, cunning, heartless creature! It is a shame to be your son! You are so venomous that you have trapped the king with your promise. Did you think that I would rejoice on getting the crown? Don't you know that Rama is everything to me? If only you were not my mother, I would have killed you. Also, my brother, Rama would not allow me to do that. You deserve to die a horrible death, you wretched woman!"

He then rushed to Kausalya's room to ask her for forgiveness. Kausalya, distressed to the core, received him with affection and said, "Bharatha, your mother has secured the kingdom for you. Go and get yourself crowned!"

Deeply wounded by her words, Bharatha fell on her feet and cried, "Mother, please do not hurt me anymore. I did a blunder by leaving the kingdom for some time. So much has happened here without my knowledge. I am deprived of my father and my beloved brothers. What more

sorrow do I want? Mother, I can never accept the crown. It belongs to brother Rama and no one else!"

Moved by his words, Kausalya hugged him and consoled him. She understood that neither he knew nor was he a part of Kaikeyi's evil scheme.

Vasishtha then reminded Bharatha that Dasaratha's funeral rites had to be arranged. With a heavy heart, Bharatha followed him.

Meanwhile, after crossing the Ganga, Rama bid farewell to Guha. The three walked deep into the forest and reached Sage Bharadwaja's hermitage who was pleased to have them. He then advised Rama to set up his hermitage at the Chitrakoota Mountains. The trio received the sage's blessings and proceeded to Chitrakoota where Lakshmana made a hut.

Meeting of the Brothers

In the meantime, Bharatha expressed his wish to Vasishtha, to bring Rama back and crown him as the king of Ayodhya. Vasishtha too welcomed his decision. Thus, Bharatha, Shatrugna, the ministers, the army, the queen mothers and even the people, went in search of Rama.

When Guha saw the army and Bharatha's flag from the other side of the river, he thought that they had come to attack Rama. But Bharatha ran and hugged him and said, "Friend, please tell me where Bharadwaja's hermitage is? We have come to take his guidance." Still doubtful, Guha said, "I would definitely tell you. But, please tell me, why have you brought such a massive army with you? Do you intend to harm Rama?"

Bharatha shuddered, "No, dear friend. I am Rama's brother, Bharatha. He is like my father. I want him to return to Ayodhya and be the king."

Guha was very sorry for his misunderstanding and escorted Bharatha's entourage to Bharadwaja's hermitage.

At Chitrakoota, Lakshmana who was keeping a watch saw Bharatha with people coming towards them. Agitated, he told Rama, "O brother, Bharatha is coming with a large army to attack us. He is coming to make sure that you don't return to claim his kingdom. I shall not leave him now. Give me your orders!"

Rama calmed him down while Bharatha came running towards him with folded hands, and fell at Rama's feet sobbing, "Forgive me, brother!" Rama lifted him, hugged and consoled him. He said, "Bharatha, why did you leave our father and come here?"

Bharatha burst out, "Brother! Our father is no more. He died as he could not hold the grief of your separation!"

These words shocked Rama who broke down in silence. Bharatha continued, "Brother, I beg you to return to Ayodhya and take the crown. Let me, in your place, go to the forest and keep our father's promise. See, I have brought everyone to persuade you." Rama then saw Sage Vasishtha, the queen mothers and Shatrugna, standing at some distance.

Rama offered his salutations to them and continued, "Brother, our father wished exile for me for fourteen years, and the throne for you. Is it not our duty to obey our father? We cannot dishonour his words."

Vasishtha, who had been watching them declared, "Bharatha, Rama is right. Rule the kingdom on Rama's behalf for fourteen years. That way, Rama would still be the king, and your father's words would also be honoured."

Bharatha agreed to rule on behalf of Rama but said, "If Rama does not come back at the end of fourteen years, I will immolate myself." Then, turning to Rama, he said, "Brother, please give me your sandals. I will place them on the throne for the next fourteen years. I would serve them as I serve you."

Rama gave his sandals, which Bharatha carried on his head as the highest honour for his brother Rama, and reached Ayodhya.

At the Dandaka Forest

After Bharatha and his entourage left, Rama thought that living closer to Ayodhya would make people visit him often and that would dilute the purpose of his renunciation. So, he decided to move away from Chitrakoota. The trio went to the hermitage of Sage Atri, who welcomed them. Sita sought the blessings of his wife, Anasuya, who preached her about the duties of a chaste woman. Thereafter, they left, with Sita walking in between Rama and Lakshmana.

As they were enjoying the beauty of the forests and walking ahead, they came across the monstrous forest-demon, Viradha. Rama and Lakshmana relieved him from the curse and proceeded to the hermitage of Sage Agastya. He blessed Rama and gave him Vishnu's bow crafted by the celestial craftsman, Vishwakarma. He also gave him a quiver of arrows and a sword and said, "With these weapons given to me by Vishnu, you have to destroy all the demons that are a terror to all of us. That will be your mission." On his advice, the trio proceeded to Panchavati situated on the banks of River Godavari.

On their way, they came across Jatayu, the Great Eagle, perched on a rock. Jatayu bowed to Rama. Sita was frightened when she saw such a huge eagle. Jatayu then told Rama that he had been a great friend of King Dasaratha. He promised to take

upon the task of protecting them as long as they were in Panchavati. He then said, "While I fly, follow me in the shadow of my wings."

Once at Panchavati, Rama, Sita and Lakshmana were enthralled by its beautiful surroundings. Lakshmana built a hut and the three seemed to be happily settled for the whole of their exile. But, one day, Soorpanakha, the widowed sister of Ravana arrived, enamored by the charm of Rama. She took the form of a damsel and said to Rama, "O handsome! I want to marry you. Will you marry me?"

Rama too was struck by her beauty. He told her, "Oh beautiful! I am already married." Then, pointing to Lakshmana, he said, "There! That is my brother. You can approach him with your proposal."

Soorpanakha then went to Lakshmana and said, "O handsome prince! I want to marry you."

Lakshmana thought he could continue the same way as Rama did. He said, "I heard that you are a princess. I am a servant of Prince Rama. So for your status, I will be too low." Soorpanakha went back to Rama and saw Sita beside him. She said, "Oh! This is your wife! Is she more beautiful than me? You don't want to marry me because of her. Let me remove her from here." Saying thus, Soorpanakha pounced upon Sita. Lakshmana who had been watching this from a distance, got Rama's signal and chopped Soorpanakha's nose. Howling in deep pain, Soorpanakha fled into the forest to her cousins Khara and Dooshana.

At the Ravana's Palace

Khara and Dooshana were alarmed at her sight and agitatedly asked what had happened.

Soorpanakha said, "Brothers! Two humans, Rama and Lakshmana, the princes of Ayodhya have come to Panchavati as ascetics. There is also a woman with them!" She explained how she had been mutilated and persuaded her cousins to avenge the terrible insult she had received. She further said, "If you really care for me, go and slay them. Bring me their blood!"

Khara and Dooshana sent their army towards Panchavati. When Rama saw their army approaching, he instructed Lakshmana to take Sita to a safer place. When that was done, Rama single-handedly faced the entire army and wiped them out.

Hearing about the defeat, Khara and Dooshana now decided to encounter Rama with their army of the most powerful 'rakshasas.' The army reached Panchavati and surrounded Rama's ashram. With least effort, Rama again defeated Khara, Dooshana and their army. Seeing their plight, Soorpanakha fled to Lanka to her brother, Ravana.

The entry of Soorpanakha brought an absolute silence in the court. Ravana's wrath knew no bounds and he thundered to her, "What is this? Who did this to you?"

Soorpanakha told him about Rama, saying, "Brother! Words cannot describe the beauty and valour of the prince. He has wiped out our entire army singlehanded! Not only is he handsome, but also the woman who is with him is a divine beauty, a damsel, in the true sense. Her name is Sita. Certainly you deserve her! I thought of bringing her to you but Rama's brother interfered and severed my nose."

Having heard so much about Sita from his sister, Ravana started picturizing Sita in his mind's eyes. He felt restless and uneasy, and started plotting on how to bring Sita to his palace.

He summoned Maricha and handed him over the mission to bring Sita to him. Maricha, who had seen the strength of Rama already and having left his bad old behaviour, advised Ravana, "No, it is better to keep away from Rama. He is very powerful. And thinking of abducting another man's wife is not right. It is immoral!"

Ravana insisted, "Maricha, think about Soorpanakha! Should we not take revenge upon Rama for what he has done to her? Rama should be deprived of his beloved. Now, I've had enough of your advice. Just do what I have asked you to."

When he found that it was beyond him to convince Ravana, Maricha agreed,

"I will do as you wish. But I am warning you of a greater danger in fighting Rama." Ravana ignored his words and said, "Take the form of a golden deer and go to Rama's hermitage. I'll do the rest."

At Panchavati, Sita and Rama were enjoying the beautiful surroundings, when Sita spotted the golden deer, Maricha. Enchanted by its beauty, she told Rama, "My dear lord! How beautiful that deer is! Can you bring it for me?"

But Lakshmana stopped him, "Brother! I don't think it is a real deer. It must be a mischief of some rakshasa."

But Sita insisted Rama to get the golden deer.

As Rama could not refuse Sita, he decided to get the golden deer.

The Abduction and the Search

Before leaving, Rama instructed Lakshmana, "Brother! I am going to look for the golden deer. Take care of Sita in my absence and do not leave her alone in any case."

Lakshmana bowed to his brother and promised to do as asked. Rama ran in the direction of the deer and when he saw it, the deer started running, deeper and deeper into the forest. Rama decided to kill it and shot an arrow which pierced the deer.

The next moment, the deer turned into Maricha, who imitated Rama's voice and screamed, "Lakshmana! Sita! Help me!"

Sita was inside the hut and when she heard him, she became agitated and insisted Lakshmana to go and look for Rama.

Knowing that it could be the trick of a rakshasa, Lakshmana tried to assure her of Rama's safety.

However, when Sita persisted that he should go and save Rama, Lakshmana drew a boundary line outside their hut and told Sita, "Mother! Please do not step beyond this line or you may get into danger."

Ravana, who had been watching Lakshmana leave Sita, took the guise of a sage and approached her. He bowed to her and asked her for alms. At once, Sita brought some food and tried to give it to the sage without crossing the line Lakshmana had drawn. However, Ravana persuaded her to cross the line. When she did that the sage quickly turned to his original form – Ravana and with a wicked laugh said, "I am Ravana, the king of Lanka. I have come to take you with me. I will make you my queen."

Sita angrily replied, "You cunning man! How dare you talk to me like that! My husband will be here now! Face him if you are brave enough."

Enraged, Ravana caught hold of her, flung her into his chariot and flew up in the sky. Sita started crying loudly, "O my lord! Where are you? Please come back !" There was no reply. Jatayu, the king of birds, who was seated high up on a tree, saw Ravana holding her and immediately recognized Sita.

He tried to stop Ravana and appealed, "Ravana! You are a king! How shameful of you to abduct another man's wife! Rama is a great warrior. If you are afraid of encountering him, leave Sita, and go away before he sees you!" Ravana was not at all affected by his words and threatened to kill the old

creature.
When
Jatayu hit
Ravana with
his wings,
the latter lost
his temper and
chopped off Jatayu's
wings. Jatayu fell down
bleeding profusely, but held his breath, hoping to
meet Rama.

While the chariot was flying away with Ravana
and Sita towards Lanka, Sita was looking down for
her beloved. She saw some monkeys sitting on a
hilltop. An idea struck her mind. She removed her
ornaments one by one and threw them down all
along the way.

Rama and Lakshmana, having done with
Maricha, came back to their hut and found Sita
missing. Feeling saddened by the events, they
started searching for her and finally reached the
spot where Jatayu lay bleeding.

Rama rushed to Jatayu and asked him about
the cause of his injury. Jatayu gave him a detailed
account of the abduction of Sita by Ravana. Then,
when he breathed his last, Rama performed the last
rites for him.

Rama's Meeting with Sugreeva

Rama and Lakshmana proceeded their journey in search of Sita, and reached the mountain abode of King Sugreeva, the exiled brother of Bali. He was assisted by his minister, Jambhavan and Hanuman. Sugreeva saw Rama and Lakshmana and thought his brother Bali had sent them to spy on him. Bali had usurped Sugreev's kingdom of Kishkinda, and had driven him off to exile.

He sent Hanuman to confront them. Hanuman bowed to the brothers, introduced himself and asked about their mission. Rama said, "Ravana, the king of Lanka has abducted my wife Sita and carried her to his palace. We are searching for her."

Hanuman was overjoyed to meet Rama. He prostrated before them and said, "My lord! I am honoured by your presence here. I am at your service. I would beg you to meet our king Sugreeva who would help you in looking for mother Sita."

He carried them on his shoulders to meet Sugreeva, who too was pleased to see Rama. After an exchange of greetings, Sugreeva asked Rama about his mission and Rama told him about Sita's abduction.

While they were talking, Sugreeva showed Rama

a bundle which had Sita's jewels. He told Rama that some of his 'Vanaras' had come across those jewels, and asked him if they belonged to Mother Sita. Rama looked at the jewels and he was moved to tears being reminded of Sita.

Hanuman related Sugreeva's story about how his brother took his throne forcefully and also his wife. Rama promised to help Sugreeva by fighting Bali and restoring his throne and wife. While in return, Sugreeva assured about his help in finding Sita.

Sugreeva was doubtful about the strength of Rama, against the indomitable powers of his brother. Bali could pluck huge trees with bare hands as if they were just blades of grass. Rama understood that Sugreeva was not convinced of his strength, so he decided to show Sugreeva his skill at archery. He shot an arrow which went straight, piercing several trees in succession, then through the seven worlds and the seven seas, before returning to his quiver. Astounded by this display, Sugreeva bowed to Rama in humility having understood Rama's prowess.

Rama asked Sugreeva to invite Bali for a fight. Though Bali agreed, his wife, Tara warned him about the supreme powers of Rama and Lakshmana but Bali ignored her and proceeded, well equipped to fight Sugreeva.

A fierce fight started between the two brothers, while Rama hid behind a tree. He was almost ready to shoot his arrow when suddenly he became confused about who Sugreeva was, for the two brothers looked the same.

Meanwhile, Bali showed all his powers to fight Sugreeva, who, being badly injured went back to Rama and said, "Rama, you did not attack Bali as you had promised!" Rama told him calmly that he could not distinguish between the two brothers. Then he handed over a garland to Sugreeva and said, "Wear this garland around your neck so that I can identify you." Sugreeva agreed, and once again called Bali for a fight. Now Rama shot his arrow at Bali, who fell down on the ground injured.

Vanar Sena Sets into Action

As he lay dying, Bali saw Rama behind the tree. He got the divine realization about Rama being the incarnation of Lord Vishnu. With folded hands, he said, "Rama, did you do that mean act of killing me by hiding? You, the protector of creatures, what you have done is not righteous. You, a great warrior, did not act in accordance to Kshatriya Dharma."

Rama explained, "Bali, you forcefully took your brother's kingdom and also his wife, which is an immoral act. I gave my word to Sugreeva about helping him defeat you. And he in return, he promised me to bring back my wife, Sita from Ravana."

Bali now said, "Did you then kill me to favour Sugreeva? You could have asked for my help in bringing Sita from Ravana by killing him. Just a word from you, and I would have brought him hurling down to your feet. Instead, you chose to kill a man who was unarmed!"

Rama calmly convinced him about his promise.

Bali, having understood Rama's predicament, bowed and said, "O Lord! I feel blessed to have died by your hands." He then instructed Sugreeva

to take care of the kingdom and also his family and Bali breathed his last.

After the last rites of Bali were performed, Sugreeva was crowned as the king in elaborate rituals. Then, he told Rama, "O Lord! Now I am ready to serve you. Command me what my duty is!"

Rama said, "Sugreeva! Now as a king, your first duty is towards your kingdom. We will wait till the monsoons are over and then I will take your help."

However, after the season ended, Sugreeva did not turn up. Lakshmana was anxious and angry. He took Rama's permission and went to meet Sugreeva at his palace. Sugreeva calmed him down and assured him of his help and then proceeded to meet Rama. In his presence, Sugreeva called all his commanders – Jambhavan , Hanuman, Nal and Neel and assigned them the task of searching for Sita in different directions.

Hanuman and his army of 'vanaras' (monkeys) were sent southwards to search for Sita. They were given a month's time to come back with some good news about finding Sita. Rama handed over his ring to

Hanuman and said, "Give this to Sita. She will know that you are my messenger."

The Vanara group headed by Hanuman searched every forest, mountain and desert, and reached a cave exhausted. It was an enchanted cave that went deep into the underworld and further led to a beautiful city whose streets were paved with gold and trees full of fresh fruits. A woman was seen meditating. She was Swayamprabha who had been condemned to this lonely place by a curse. With the entry of Hanuman and his army, her long penance had ended. Hanuman narrated his mission and was told, "Noble creatures, whoever enters the cave cannot leave the place alive, but since you are on a noble mission, I will transport you to the real world."

The next moment, Hanuman and his army found themselves in the real world. Just below them, they found a vast expanse of ocean.

Hanuman Reaches Lanka

Having searched for Sita in every nook and corner, Hanuman and his army, exhausted all their hopes. Angada reminded Hanuman that the one month time given by Sugreeva had ended and they were yet to make a breakthrough in their mission. At this Hanuman said, "Angada, we should not give up so easily. Let us sing the praise of Rama and pray him to give us victory in our mission. Long live Rama!" The others too joined Hanuman.

At a little distance from them Sampathi, an old vulture, the brother of Jatayu was standing. When he heard about Jatayu's death he started crying. He then went to Hanuman and introduced himself as the elder brother of Jatayu and said. "We were separated long ago. I did not know about his whereabouts. But now you say he is dead. I was told that my redemption would be in the hands of Rama, the noble prince, the incarnation of God on earth. As you have mentioned the name of Rama, I feel that I will meet him very soon. Tell me what brings you all here?"

Hanuman related to him about Ravana's abduction of Sita, Jatayu's noble sacrifice, and Rama and Lakshmana's inability to locate her place.

Then Sampathi said, "Oh, yes, yes! A few months ago I saw a golden chariot flying above this mountain top. It was Ravana and the woman must have been Sita. They went to the other side of this ocean where Ravana's kingdom lies." Then Sampathi, who had very sharp eyesight, looked across the ocean and assured Hanuman, "Look there! I can see the city of Lanka. Such a beautiful city with tall, huge buildings and magnificent fortress! I can even see the thick Ashoka Vatika. And there she is! Mother Sita sitting under the tree, surrounded by hideous 'rakshasis'!"

Sampathi's words brought an excitement and a new hope in the disheartened 'Vanara' Army headed by Hanuman. Sampathi then wished them good luck and left.

Left to themselves, the Vanara Army started discussing as to who would do the big task of leaping across the ocean. Jambhavan, the bear, who was the oldest among them said, "Hanuman, I think you are the most suited for this task. Your strength is equivalent to Sugreeva, and even Rama and Lakshmana. You have the ability to increase your size according to your wish and only you can do this work." Everyone's eyes looked up to Hanuman.

Hanuman took his blessings and started his

journey across the ocean. He took a big leap and reached Mount Mahendra. Now he took a jump over the huge ocean. He was flying over the ocean when Mount Mainak sprung into air to give him rest. Half way across the ocean, a rakshasi emerged and tried to swallow him. As she opened her mouth, Hanuman magnified his size, according to which the rakshasi too opened her mouth wider and wider. Then, Hanuman quickly shrank his size as tiny as a speck, entered into her mouth and came out the next instance, before she could react. The next moment, the rakshasi turned into a beautiful woman. She was Surasa who had been sent by the Gods to test Hanuman's cleverness. She blessed Hanuman who then finally reached Lanka.

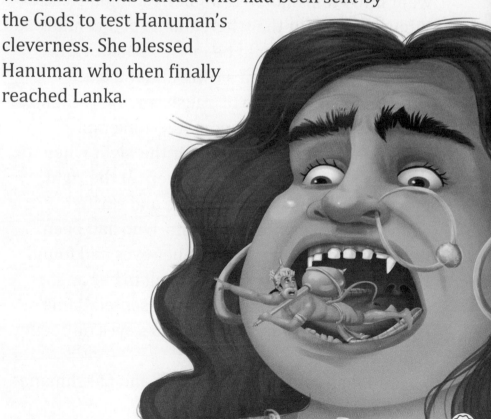

Smoldering of Lanka

After crossing the ocean, Hanuman landed on the sands of Lanka. He peeped into the buildings in search of Sita and then looked into Ravana's palace. He remembered Sampathi's words that mother Sita would be found at the Ashoka Vatika. As he was moving towards it, he heard the name of Rama being chanted. He stopped and looked through the window of the chamber from where he had heard the chanting and saw Ravana's brother, Vibhishana.

Hanuman took the form of a Brahmin and went into Vibhishana's chamber. Hanuman asked Vibhishana about the whereabouts of Sita and was assured that Sita would be in the Ashoka Vatika.

Hanuman found Sita sitting under a tree, surrounded by a group of 'rakshasis.' He recognized her and was pained by her state – unkempt and undecorated. He waited for the night when the rakshasis would go off to sleep. At the right moment, he came down the tree and started chanting the name of Rama. Sita, who had been thinking about Rama, opened her eyes and found Hanuman, who introduced himself to her and narrated his mission. Then, he presented Rama's ring to her. Tears flowed from Sita's eyes on seeing Rama's ring.

Hanuman said, "Mother! Rama and Lakshmana

would come here very soon to kill Ravana and destroy Lanka but before that, please give me the honour of carrying you across the sea on my shoulders to Rama." Sita replied, "O son of Vayu. I know your strength. But if you carry me on your shoulders, it would be a dishonor to noble Rama. Let my Lord come here as a noble warrior, defeat Ravana and take me away!"

Hanuman bowed to her and said, "Hey mother, what proof would I then give to our lord Rama that I met you?" Sita gave a piece of her jewel to Hanuman and said, " Vayuputra! Give this to my lord as a proof."

As he left Sita, Hanuman started rampaging the garden. News had already reached Ravana, and Indrajit who rushed to capture Hanuman. He then took him to Ravana's court, where Hanuman coiled his tail in the form of a seat, higher than that of Ravana and sat on it. His audacity enraged Ravana, who ordered his men to set fire to Hanuman's tail. When this news had reached Sita, she prayed to God Agni "O Agnidev! Have mercy on Hanuman. Do not harm him with your heat!" Thus, the fire set on Hanuman's tail did not harm him. He started leaping from one building to another, setting fire to everything that had come in his tail's way. Everything, except the Ashoka Vatika was charred, after which, Hanuman went to the sea to put out the fire from his tail.

Preparation for the Battle

Hanuman returned to Kishkinda and met Rama. Before Rama could ask any question, an exulted Hanuman said, "I've seen Mother Sita, O Lord!" This was great news for Rama. Then Hanuman handed him the jewel that Sita had given. Rama embraced him as a mark of gratitude. Thereafter, Rama and Sugreeva started making their plan– to defeat Ravana and bring back Sita.

At Lanka, Ravana too was scared of the rampage created by Hanuman. He called his ministers to seek their counsel and suggestions. Kumbhakarna, Ravana's brother, Indrajit and Vibhishana were all present there. While Kumbhakarna gave assurance to Ravana about their formidable position against Rama, Vibhishana said, "Brother! Don't have high hopes about defeating Rama. You were wrong in abducting another man's wife. Rama is a mighty and noble warrior. Let us free Sita, so that she can go to Rama and we can seek his pardon."

These words added fire to Ravana's fury and he said with contempt, "Worthless brother! How can you admire Rama? He is our enemy. I am sparing you as you are my brother."

Shattered by these words, Vibhishana bowed to his brother, Ravana and said, "I plead you, brother to reconsider your idea to set a war against Rama. If you still persist, I can just pray to God to give you good sense."

Ravana said with a raised voice, "Vibhishana, don't provoke me! Just go away from my sight. You have no place here, in my kingdom."

Vibhishana now felt that it was of no use to persuade his brother and decided that his only refuge would be Rama. Thus, he crossed the seas and reached Rama's camp on the other shore, where the Vanara Army had gathered. They first mistook Vibhishana to be a spy from the enemy army. The news of his arrival reached Sugreeva. He too was doubtful and met Rama to whom he said, "Hey Rama! At this point, we cannot trust anyone. He seems to be a spy from the Ravana camp. Give us your orders to kill him." Angada too joined him

while Jambhavan aired his opinion, "Rama, you know very well from your earlier experiences that the rakshasas are known for their cunningness. It is a risk to admit any one from the enemy camp."

Rama listened to them patiently but reacted differently. He assured them, "I do agree with you all. My safety is of prime importance to you. But even if he comes as an enemy, I would welcome him."

Hanuman, who was listening to them, welcomed the idea and said, "O Lord! Although, he is Ravana's brother, I don't think he has come here as a spy. I find him to be righteous. Therefore, I too think that we should invite him cordially."

As Vibhishana was taken inside, he fell at Rama's feet and uttered, "O Lord! I am pleased to meet you. I am Ravana's brother but still I have come here to seek your refuge. Please accept me in your camp." Rama touched his shoulder, embraced him and told him that he would be safe with Rama. He also crowned Vibhishana then and there as the King of Lanka.

The Bridge across the Sea

After being crowned as the king, Vibhishana assured Rama that it was not his purpose of coming to Rama. He wanted the lord's grace on him. He requested Rama to include him in the war council. That being done, Vibhishana revealed all important secrets about Lanka's defences: Ravana's troops, his weapons and the strength of his army which helped Rama to plan his attack on Lanka.

The next step was to cross over the sea. Rama prayed to the Sea God day and night for seven days after which the Sea God appeared before him. Rama bowed to the God and said, "Please make way for my army to go across!"

But the Sea God said, "Rama, I cannot go against the laws of nature." Frustrated, Rama threatened to shoot his arrows into the sea so that all the waters would evaporate and make way for him and his armies. Thereupon, the Sea God requested him to calm down and advised him to build a bridge over the sea.

The Vanaras got into action, uprooting big trees and bringing huge rocks to the shore, under the supervision of Nal and Neel, the architects. Soon, the 'Ram Setu' began to get shape. At Lanka, the news had reached Ravana about the arrival of the Vanara Army. He deployed his armies from all the corners of the city and entrusted important roles to his generals and kinsmen.

As for Rama, he felt that he could give one last chance to Ravana to mend his ways. So, he sent Angada as his messenger to Ravana, who alerted him, "Ravana, you know that our troops have landed in Lanka, and we are sure to win. Do not invite death upon yourself. Return Sita to the noble Rama who forgives even his enemies. Also, mind that your brother, Vibhishana, has joined our army and has already been crowned the king of Lanka. If you still choose to be stubborn, your arrogance would bring your doom."

A relentless Ravana got angry at these words and ordered his men to seize Angada, who in turn, attacked them and returned safely to Rama. Rama was now sure that war was inevitable and ordered his army to charge at Ravana's army.

Ravana, in the meantime, felt that he had to somehow persuade Sita into marrying him, lest she would be taken away by Rama. He took an illusory head of Rama in a tray and showed it to Sita, saying, "See what has happened to your Rama! You did not yield to my wishes so I have beheaded Rama and here's the proof! Come on, now you have no other option. You have to be my queen."

Shocked at the sight of the illusory head, Sita swooned. Trijata, one of the rakshasis, who was guarding Sita, had a soft corner for her. She consoled her saying, "This is definitely not Rama's head. I know Ravana's cunningness. He is doing this to persuade you. Your Rama is very much safe and has arrived with a huge Vanara Army to Lanka to attack Ravana. Very soon, he will take you away." These words soothed Sita.

The War and the Result

As soon as the Vanara Army landed on the shores of Lanka, it charged at the rakshasas with uprooted trees and big boulders but were retaliated with weapons. Then followed individual attacks between warriors of both sides. At one point, Indrajit, the son of Ravana, bound Rama and Lakshmana with his deadly 'Nagapasha' or the serpent dart. The brothers swooned while their enemies rejoiced. However, Garuda, the Divine Eagle, landed up in time to rescue and recuperate the brothers. Seeing him, the serpents moved away in fear. Both Rama and Lakshmana sat up and were blessed by Garuda before he flew away.

Ravana began to send his commanders one by one but lost them all. Now finding the situation beyond control, Ravana himself decided to fight in the battle field. After killing many Vanaras, he encountered Rama, who, riding on Hanuman's back, retaliated. What followed was a fierce battle. Both fought till Ravana's weapons had been exhausted and his chariot destroyed. Ravana stood helpless and unarmed in front of Rama.

The righteous Rama however said to Ravana, "You are a great warrior. Go back today and come tomorrow!" Humiliated and crestfallen, Ravana went to wake up his brother, Kumbakarna, who he thought, would be enough to smash the entire Vanara Army at one shot.

Kumbhakarna reached the battle field for the love of his brother. When the Vanaras saw the massive mountain like figure of Kumbhakarna, they started losing heart and ran helter-skelter in terror. Angada instilled confidence in them and all the Vanaras attacked Kumbhakarna in unison but he remained sturdy. Finally, Rama shot a powerful arrow and severed the head of Kumbhakarna. Ravana was now devastated as he had lost his brother.

Indrajit, the son of Ravana, then marched to the battlefield with his troops. After a long battle, he released his 'Brahmastra' on Lakshmana, who fell unconscious on the field. Jambhavan suggested Hanuman to bring the 'medicinal herbs' from Mount Sanjeevani. On landing up there, Hanuman was confused about the medicinal herb so he lifted the entire hill and flew back to Lanka. Lakshmana was administered the medicine and was healed soon.

There was much rejoicing in Rama's camp. Disheartened Indrajit started performing a yagna, the success of which would make him invincible. When Vibhishana told Rama about this, he sent Lakshmana with Hanuman and other Vanaras to stop Indrajit. A fierce battle followed and Lakshmana, standing on Hanuman's shoulder fought Indrajit and beheaded him using Indrastra.

Left with no more warriors, Ravana headed to the field for the second time. What followed was a bloody battle; with Ravana energized by the thirst for revenge against Rama and his troops.

The Gods who were watching the fight from Heaven asked Indra to help Rama. Thus, Indra sent his celestial chariot and charioteer Matali to help Rama.

In the meantime, Matali approached Rama and advised him to use his Brahmastra. Vibhishana informed Rama that Ravana's immortality lay in his navel. When Rama shot the Brahmastra at his navel, Ravana fell dead. The Vanara Army went into a wild ecstasy. The deities from the heaven showered flowers upon Rama for his ultimate victory over evil.

Return to Ayodhya and Rama's Coronation

After the defeat of Ravana, Rama sent Hanuman to fetch Sita, who had already got the news of Rama's victory. She was overjoyed to hear the news. Hanuman then reached the Ashoka Vatika and after paying his respects to Sita, requested her to present herself before Rama. She was taken in a palanquin to meet Rama. Both wept on seeing each other.

Rama then told her, "Sita, I have killed Ravana, not only to claim you back, but for a higher cause. I have done the duty as a Kshatriya. It was also a fulfillment of the promise that I had made to the sages. But, I cannot accept you. As a married woman, you have stayed at a stranger's place for a year. Therefore, I want you to undergo a chastity test to prove your purity."

Sita broke down and asked, "O my Lord, I thought your victory would bring an end to all my trials. But you doubt my chastity. What else can I want? I will do whatever you want me to do!"

Then turning to Lakshmana, she said, "Lakshmana, light a fire at once." A helpless Lakshmana went about the task and kindled a fire. Sita invoked the God of Fire and prayed, "O Agnidev! You are the witness to my purity. Take me into your folds." Then, she went round Rama thrice and then the fire thrice, after which, she stepped into it. Miraculously, the fire did not harm her. From its heart, rose the Fire God, who held Sita aloft and handed her over to Rama saying, "Rama! Sita is pure and chaste. Accept her!" Thereupon, the Gods and the Goddesses from the heaven showered their blessings on the divine couple.

With just a few days left for the end of their fourteen years exile, Rama made arrangements to return back to Ayodhya. Under his instruction, a Pushpaka Vimana (flying chariot) was arranged

onto which Rama, Lakshmana, Sita, Hanuman, Sugreeva and Vibhishana mounted. They were flown to Ayodhya and landed at the Dandaka forest to receive the blessings of Sage Agastya. Then, they all went to Chitrakoota where Rama gave instructions to Hanuman to inform Bharatha about his arrival.

When Bharatha got the information, he came running to meet Rama and was overwhelmed to see his brother. He said with folded hands to Rama, "Brother, here's your crown. I have faithfully served the kingdom, and now I want to be relieved from my responsibility." Rama embraced Bharatha.

The coronation ceremony was duly arranged. Rama and Sita were flanked by Bharatha, Lakshmana and Shatrugna. Sugreeva and Vibhishana gently fanned them, while Hanuman sat down at Rama's feet. The entire Ayodhya was present to attend the ceremony. The Gods from the heavens showered flowers over them and the sages chanted holy hymns. Sage Vasishtha and the queens blessed Rama.

Rama ruled the kingdom righteously. There  was peace and prosperity in the land. It was an ideal administration and came to be known as 'Rama Rajya'.